HARVINGTON HALL

PHOTOGRAPHIC MEMORIES

For the Millennium, the Hall held an exhibition of comparative photographs of Harvington Hall. One set had been taken at the turn of the 19th and 20th centuries, the other at the turn of the 20th and 21st centuries.

The photographs are now on display in appropriate rooms in the Hall; some of the photographs are reproduced in this book, which was compiled by the Hall Manager, **SHERIDA BREEDEN.**

A qualified teacher, with two daughters, Sherida has worked at the Hall since 1998. She felt that although the Hall's early history in the 16th and 17th centuries is fascinating, its more recent rescue from the ravages of time and neglect is also worth recording – hence this book.

HARVINGTON HALL

PHOTOGRAPHIC MEMORIES

SHERIDA BREEDEN

First published in the United Kingdom in 2005
by Black Horse Books, an imprint of The Francis Frith Collection

British Library Cataloguing in Publication Data

Harvington Hall Photographic Memories
Sherida Breeden
ISBN 1-84546-330-7

Produced exclusively by The Francis Frith Collection for:
Harvington Hall
Kidderminster
Worcestershire DY10 4LR

The Francis Frith Collection
Frith's Barn, Teffont,
Salisbury, Wiltshire SP3 5QP
Tel: +44 (0) 1722 716 376
Email: info@francisfrith.co.uk
www.francisfrith.co.uk

Printed and bound in Great Britain

Front Cover: **KIDDERMINSTER**, *Harvington Hall c1918* zzz03213k
*The colour-tinting is for illustrative purposes only, and is not intended to be
historically accurate*

Aerial photographs reproduced under licence from
Simmons Aerofilms Limited.
Historical Ordnance Survey maps reproduced under licence from
Homecheck.co.uk

Every attempt has been made to contact copyright holders of illustrative
material. We will be happy to give full acknowledegement in future
editions for any items not credited. Any information should be directed to
Sherida Breeden at Harvington Hall.

CONTENTS

HARVINGTON HALL
PREFACE

MANY BOOKS have been written about the early life of Harvington Hall: its origins as a small medieval manor house, extensively rebuilt in the reign of Elizabeth I; its turbulent history as the home of the recusant Catholic family of Humphrey and Abigail Pakington; and its life over the succeeding four centuries. This book, however, is a pictorial record of the last 100 years or so at the Hall.

Left: **HARVINGTON HALL** *2000* ZZZ03215

Above: **HARVINGTON HALL** *1957* K16065 (THE FRANCIS FRITH COLLECTION©)

**HARVINGTON HALL
FROM THE AIR**
*1953 (Simmons Aerofilm
Limited)* AFR 19119

HARVINGTON HALL
c1960 K16066 (THE FRANCIS
FRITH COLLECTION©)

The view of the back
garden across the moat,
the Georgian chapel on
the left and the Malt
House on the right.

11

THE HALL BEFORE 1900

THE PRESENT DAY Hall is built on the site of a medieval 14th-century house, basically H-shaped, of timber framing on a sandstone foundation, with a stone tiled roof. This was the home of the de Harvingtons. The house eventually passed to Thomas Beauchamp, Earl of Warwick, and for nearly two centuries after that it formed part of the estates of the successive Earls of Warwick.

In 1529 it was sold to John Pakington, a wealthy lawyer who was later knighted by Henry VIII. It was his nephew, another John Pakington, who began the present house just before his death in 1578, but the first record of anyone living at Harvington Hall refers to his son, Humphrey, in 1582-83. Much of the Elizabethan re-building which you see today was his work.

Some parts of the medieval house were kept, but encased in brick, and large additions were constructed on four sides of the courtyard, using local sandstone for foundations, quoins and dressings. The sandstone came from the little quarry along the lane, and the bricks were made in a brick kiln in the fields behind the southwest corner of the island.

Harvington Hall is famous for its rare wall paintings and for the greatest number of existing priests' hiding places in the country, both legacies from the days of Humphrey Pakington. In the 1590s the country under Elizabeth I was Protestant, but Humphrey and his family followed the Catholic faith. Taking advantage of the fact that a new staircase was being installed in about 1600, several ingenious hides, possibly by the famous hide maker Nicholas Owen, were incorporated into the Hall. Because no one was ever found in any of these hides, they remained as they were, forgotten and neglected over the centuries, providing us today with a fascinating insight into the religious persecution of the time.

The Hall passed to Humphrey's daughter, Mary, who had married John Yate, and then eventually to her granddaughter Mary, who was the wife of Sir Robert Throckmorton. The Hall was owned by the Throckmorton family right up until the beginning of the 20th century.

Mary and Robert Throckmorton demolished two sides of the Hall around the courtyard, probably in 1701, the date on the lead rainwater head in the courtyard; by this time the Throckmorton family had other properties at Buckland in Devon and Coughton in Warwickshire, and the Hall was used only by bailiffs and the parish priest. Many of the rooms ceased to be used, and letters of the early 1800s describe the leaking roofs, damp and rats, painting a picture of the onset of decay and desolation.

THE LEAD RAINWATER HEAD zzz03217

This rainwater head can be found in the courtyard. Notice the evidence of marks made when it was used for target practice. The letters R, M and T refer to Robert and Mary Throckmorton with the date of building work - 1701.

During the 1800s much of the Hall was unfurnished; the heraldic carvings, the tapestries, the panelling and even the brass locks had been taken away by the Throckmortons for use in other properties. To add insult to injury the final blow to the old Hall was when Sir William Throckmorton took the elegant staircase, which rose from the ground floor to the third floor, and re-housed it at Coughton Court, where it can still be seen today.

THE DANCE FAMILY OUTSIDE THE HALL *c1890* zzz03221
Mrs Charlotte Dance was caretaker in the 1890s. Her son George Dance, one of the boys in this picture, went on to become a famous TT rider.

The little Georgian chapel (which had been built above the stables at the Hall in 1743, when life for Catholics eased somewhat) had ceased to be used, and had been badly damaged by fire; the parish worshipped at St Mary's Church, which had been built in 1825 across the present car park from the Hall. The priest living in the Hall at that time was Father John Brownlow, who was delighted when Sir Charles Throckmorton built the priest's house on the south side of the church at a cost of £800. It enabled him to move into a more convenient and comfortable home than the Hall had been able to offer him.

FATHER JOHN BROWNLOW *c1880* ZZZ03496

**ST MARY'S CHURCH
THE INTERIOR** *c1950* ZZZ03220

The church was built in 1825.

**ST MARY'S CHURCH
FROM THE NORTH SIDE** ZZZ03978

ST MARY'S PRESBYTERY ZZZ03219

Built in 1838 adjoining the south side of the church.

FROM 1900 TO 1910

THE HALL *c1900* ZZZ03218

By 1900, ivy, which had long been encroaching upon the old building, took firm hold and threatened to engulf the whole Hall. Windows were missing or boarded up, floors were unsafe, walls were crumbling, and roofs were open to the elements.

THE EAST FRONT ZZZ03222

Not only was the Hall engulfed in ivy but the moat was overgrown and dry in places.

THE HALL *c1960* K16067 (The Francis Frith Collection©)

By 1960 the moat contained clear, free-flowing water, and was stocked with carp.

19

Left: **THE COURTYARD VIEWED FROM THE NORTH GARDEN** ZZZ03224

Below: **THE SOUTH ELEVATION LOOKING TOWARDS THE HERB GARDEN** ZZZ03223

The small lean-to building, now demolished, was an outside toilet. Curtains can just be seen in the South Room, one of the few inhabited areas.

Opposite above: **THE MALT HOUSE AND LIVESTOCK** *c1896* ZZZ03225

Opposite below: **THE SOUTH FRONT** *c1900* ZZZ03226

Local residents pose for the photographer.

After some repairs had been made to the Georgian chapel, it was opened as the village school. A teacher's desk stood where the altar had been, the south garden was used as a playground, and thirty or so pupils attended.

One of the teachers, Mrs Maria Harris, had a room at the Hall, probably the Withdrawing Room, with an area curtained off for her bed. Later, teacher Miss Mary Kellerd used Lady Yate's Room as her bedroom.

Left: A **CERTIFICATE FOR REGULAR ATTENDANCE** ZZZ03228

Opposite above: **THE WITHDRAWING ROOM** ZZZ03229

Note the white-painted panelling and the doors to the alcoves.

Opposite below: **MISS MARY KELLERD AND HER PUPILS** *c1900*

ZZZ03227

The only residents at the end of the 19th century, apart from Miss Kellerd, were Mrs Carter, who acted as caretaker, and two poor relations of the Throckmortons, the Misses Christina and Bessie Chare, who were living in the North Tower.

Mrs Carter and her family lived in the South Room and the two adjoining rooms, which are now indoor toilets. In the garderobe in the corner of the South Room was a sink which drained into the moat, and the room had a stove to cook on and keep the family warm. The pipe from the stove pierced the plaster above the entrance door, where one of the famous wall paintings, depicting a mermaid, had been whitewashed over.

Right: **HIDING PLACE UNDER THE GARDEROBE FLOOR** *c1965* K16089

Here we see the hide in the garderobe with its original cover.

THE SOUTH ROOM ZZZ03231

The garderobe in the far left-hand corner housed the Carters' sink.

Even in those days, with the Hall in such a dilapidated state, occasional visitors still came. Mrs Carter's youngest son Thomas recalled that at the end of the 19th century, the Hall was visited by none other than Joseph Chamberlain, Mr and Mrs Stanley Baldwin, the Earl of Dudley from Witley Court, Lord Cobham from Hagley, and Bishop (later Archbishop) Ilsley of Birmingham. Guiding cannot have been easy with some rooms used as living areas, others in a state of disrepair, and a general state of decay.

Above: **THE MERMAID WALL PAINTING** zzz03230

To this day, the painting of the mermaid, although now revealed from beneath its whitewash, still displays the blocked-up hole where the stove pipe had been.

Right: **THE ATTICS** zzz03232

There is evidence that visitors also explored the Hall without a guide – graffiti in the attic areas date from the late 1800s.

FROM 1910 TO 1920

IN THE very early part of the 20th century, the Birmingham Archaeological Society had become interested in the Hall (an interest that continues today, as a member of the Archaeological Society still sits on the Hall's Management Committee). The Society's president at the time was the local antiquary John Humphreys. He was a friend of the author Bede Camm, who devoted a chapter of his 1917 book *Forgotten Shrines* to Harvington Hall. He reproduced in it some early photographs which formed an invaluable record of the appearance and condition of the Hall at the turn of the 20th century.

Above left: **THE WEST SIDE OF THE HALL** *c1900* zzz03233

Above right: **THE PICNIC AREA** *2000* zzz03234

As well as photographs taken by Benjamin Stone, a series taken by Thomas Lewis was also used in the book *Forgotten Shrines*, and a third anonymous series dated 1917 showed the roof almost hidden under ivy, floors rotting, windows broken or bricked up, plaster falling from ceilings, and the roof of the chapel held up by a rough prop between the floor and the ceiling joists.

Right: **THE GREAT CHAMBER** *c1900*

ZZZ03235

Below: **THE GREAT CHAMBER** *2000*

ZZZ03236

Left: **THE WITHDRAWING ROOM** *c1900*
ZZZ03237

Below: **THE WITHDRAWING ROOM** *2000* ZZZ03238

Above: **THE NURSERY** *c1900*
ZZZ03239

Left: **THE NURSERY** *2000* ZZZ03240

Above left: **THE GAP LEFT BY THE REMOVAL OF THE GREAT STAIRCASE** *c1917* zzz03241

Above right: **THE STAIR HIDE** *c1920* zzz03242

For comparison, see over page.

Right: **THE GREAT STAIRCASE** *2000* zzz03980

Above: **THE STAIR HIDE, CLOSED** *2000*
ZZZ03505

Left: **THE STAIR HIDE, OPEN TO REVEAL A 'PRIEST'** *2000* ZZZ03504

Above left: **THE COURTYARD** *c1900*

ZZZ03243

Below left: **THE COURTYARD** *2000*

ZZZ03497

By 1913 the little school in the Georgian chapel had closed, and the teacher's quarters in the house were taken over by Frank Owen Chambers as a weekend cottage. He produced a revised guidebook, which enjoyed a steady sale to the Hall's visitors. Meanwhile the condition of the Hall was getting worse. Despite this, the parish diary records that 200 people attended a lecture in the Great Chamber given by the Archaeological Society's John Humphreys.

The diary also records that Christmas revels were held in the Hall, with a Christmas tree, prizes and entertainment. Events such as these are hard to imagine in today's Health and Safety-conscious society. The Great Chamber is now licensed for only 60 guests; candles, revels and entertainment in a derelict house with no mains services whatsoever sounds like a recipe for disaster. However, the Hall survived!

POSTER ADVERTISING
A LECTURE BY
JOHN HUMPHREYS
1919 ZZZ03245

A LECTURE

ON

HARVINGTON HALL

WILL BE GIVEN BY

Mr. JOHN HUMPHREYS, F.S.A.,

IN THE

Banqueting Hall of the Old House,

BY THE KIND PERMISSION OF THE

REV. PHILIP ROSKELL,

ON

WEDNESDAY, OCT. 8th, 1919,

At 8 p.m.

TICKETS, 2/-, 1/-,

May be obtained from :—
 The Rev. PHILIP ROSKELL, Harvington.
 Mrs. WATTS, Sion House.
 Miss PAGE, Hillpool.

The proceeds will be given for necessary repairs to roof of the Old Hall.

Paul Hicks & Co., Printers, Broad Street, Five Ways, Birm.

THE 1920s

EVENTUALLY IN 1921 the Throckmorton family decided to sell the Hall. The auctioneers' description painted a rosier picture than could have been the reality, but the property failed to reach its reserve.

AUCTIONEERS'
PARTICULARS *1921* ZZZ03247

The Estate of Sir Wm. Throckmorton, Bart., deceased.

WORCESTERSHIRE.

Particulars with Plan

of

Valuable Freehold Agricultural Property

known as

Harvington Hall Estate

Comprising good Farm House, with extensive range of Buildings, etc., and the
Noted Historical Tudor Manor House,

"Harvington Hall,"

situate about 3 miles from Kidderminster, 5 from Bromsgrove, 6 from Stourbridge, and 16 from Birmingham; in all about

250 acres.

Also a COTTAGE (disused) and LARGE GARDEN at Woodcote Green, near Bromsgrove.

To be Sold by Auction by

NOCK & JOSELAND

at the

"LION" HOTEL, KIDDERMINSTER,

on Thursday, September 15th, 1921, at 4 p.m. punctually,

by instructions from the Executors of the late Sir N. W. G. Throckmorton, Bart., and subject to Conditions annexed hereto.

FURTHER INFORMATION may be had of Messrs. Witham, Roskell, Munster & Weld, Solicitors, 1 Gray's Inn Square, London, W.C.1; Mr. Jas. Stewart, Land Agent, Llanforda Isaf, Oswestry; or of the Auctioneers, Kidderminster and Wolverhampton.

WORCESTERSHIRE.

Particulars with Plan

of

...ngton Hall Estate,

... Kidderminster.

..., at "The Lion" Hotel, Kidderminster,
on Thursday, September 15th, 1921,
at 4 o'clock punctually.

Solicitors:
Messrs. WITHAM, ROSKELL, MUNSTER & WELD,
1 Gray's Inn Square, London, W.C.1.

Land Agent:
Mr. JAS. STEWART,
Llanforda Isaf,
Oswestry.

Auctioneers
Messrs. NOCK & JOSELAND
Bank Buildings, Kidderminster, and
48 Queen Street, Wolverhampton.

In November 1923, Mrs Ellen Ryan Ferris, a dressmaker whose clients included royalty, and whose builder brothers developed much of Kings Norton, purchased the Hall for a sum of £1,100 and presented it to the Roman Catholic Archdiocese of Birmingham. Mrs Ryan Ferris, famed for her large hats, which she made herself, and for her devotion to the church, supported the Hall until her death. She is buried in the churchyard of St Mary's, Harvington.

Mrs Ferris purchased the church, the Hall itself and the grounds within the moat; this is an area of some 2½ acres, two thirds of which is water! It was not envisaged in those days that some 80 years later there would be a desperate need for land on which to park the vehicles of the numerous Hall visitors. The Hall Farm and all the land surrounding it was sold separately.

The Archdiocese must have been thrilled with such a gift as the Hall, but understandably rather overwhelmed by the amount of work needed even to make it weatherproof. Until 1929, nothing was done, but then the decision was made that the Hall must not be allowed to sink further into the moat and ignominiously fade away.

In July 1929, to mark the Centenary of the Catholic Emancipation Act, an exhibition of recusant antiquities was held in Birmingham. Among the articles on display were the photographs taken by Benjamin Stone, and interest was once again drawn to the Hall and its perilous condition. In the same year, Thomas Leighton Williams was consecrated Archbishop of Birmingham, and he at once made the decision that the Hall must be made weatherproof.

ARCHBISHOP LEIGHTON WILLIAMS zzz03501

THE 1930s

STRUCTURAL WORK costing £2,500 was completed in early 1931. When the ivy had been stripped from the walls at the front of the Hall, the roof of the Withdrawing Room collapsed, leaving that room, the Great Chamber and the Nursery open to the elements. The main structural work, therefore, involved a new roof and rafters, rebuilt chimneys, and new flooring.

THE HALL *1929* zzz03248
This photograph, taken by Mr A D Chambers in 1929, graphically shows the result of removing the ivy.

THE HALL *c1931*

ZZZ03249

The back garden of
the Hall suffered as
the workmen began
structural repairs.

In 1931 the moat was drained and cleared, and a concrete retaining wall was constructed at the south end. All these repairs were completed so quickly that by 1931 the Hall was fit to be opened regularly to visitors, entirely at their own risk of course!

In 1930 the Archbishop had set up a committee to run the Hall and continue its restoration. (The Hall is still run today by a committee appointed by the current Archbishop). Reports of committee meetings during the 1930s listed the ongoing restoration, such as the unblocking and glazing of windows, the removal of partitions put up earlier in the century to provide bedrooms, and the provision of the tea-room, a catering kitchen and earth closets.

Above: **THE HALL** *c1931* zzz03250

Below: **THE HALL** *c1931* zzz03252

THE HALL *c1931* ZZZ03251

FATHER WHITTINGTON *c1930* ZZZ03253
Father Whittington was parish priest at the time when repairs to the Hall were being undertaken during the 1930s.

By 1936, the wall paintings, which had been hidden under coats of lime wash for centuries, were beginning to be uncovered and treated. This work was directed by Elsie Matley Moore of Greyfriars in Worcester. Miss Moore made life-size copies of the paintings when they were first revealed and had more intensity of colour than they have now. Her original paintings are held at Birmingham Museum and Art Gallery and at the Victoria & Albert Museum in London.

WALL PAINTING ABOVE THE PORCH IN THE GREAT CHAMBER ZZZ03254

Many visitors remember being told of a spy hole in a peacock's tail painted near this position, which allowed anyone hiding in the priest hide behind the painted wall to look through into the Great Chamber. There is no real evidence of a peacock in this photograph.

Right: **WALL PAINTING OF JOSHUA IN THE NINE WORTHIES PASSAGE**

ZZZ03255

Far right: **WALL PAINTING OF A CHERUB**

ZZZ03256

This cherub is one of the many that adorns the walls. One that was half way up the spiral staircase leading to the chapel at the top of the Hall, broke into fragments and fell off the wall during restoration work in the 1990s.

One of the major problems at the Hall, particularly when visitors were being shown round, was the fact that the great staircase had been removed to Coughton Court; in 1936, the decision was made to install a replica staircase up to the first floor. It was built by William Fowkes of Droitwich.

The Hall Management Committee met at least once a month at that time, and often helped with restoration work themselves, or paid for repairs out of their own pocket. The secretary of the committee from 1930 to 1951 was Henry Robert Hodgkinson, who bought Hall Farm opposite the Hall from the Throckmortons in 1934. In his own words, Henry Robert Hodgkinson 'gave or influenced' nearly all of the money subscribed for the continuing restoration; much of the furniture was donated by him through the National Trust.

The committee had to decide how to use the Hall in the future. Suggestions included a Catholic ramblers' club or a Franciscan friary. Eventually they recommended to the Archbishop that it should be a centre for devotion to John Wall, who had been declared 'Blessed' in 1929, and made a saint in 1970 and who was associated with the Hall in the 1600s.

THE STAINED GLASS WINDOW IN THE NURSERY ZZZ03257

This window depicts Lady Mary Yate and St John Wall, and was given in memory of Parish Priest Monsignor John Wall Roskell, chairman of the Management Committee from 1937 until his death in 1949.

In 1935 a 'pastoral play and pageant' about John Wall was performed in the Hall garden. Its climax had Wall swimming the moat to escape his pursuers and then riding off on horseback. The two-tier stage was erected at the end of the malthouse, and actors of all ages took part. The Hall still hosts an outdoor play each summer, but to this date such a feat has never been repeated!

Left: **HENRY ROBERT HODGKINSON** ZZZ03498

Below: **THE PASTORAL PLAY AND PAGEANT WITH A TWO-TIER STAGE CONSTRUCTED AT THE END OF THE MALT HOUSE** *1935* ZZZ03258

Right: **THE PASTORAL PLAY AND PAGEANT** *1935*

ZZZ03259

Below: **THE PASTORAL PLAY AND PAGEANT** *1935*

ZZZ03260

THE FLIGHT OF JOHN WALL *1935* zzz03261

Having swum the moat, the actor escaped on horseback followed by pursuivants!

(There are no surviving records to show that John Wall actually visited Harvington Hall)

In February 1939 a curious party was held at the Hall. Anonymous invitations from 'The Ghosts' were sent to 50 guests to attend supper with entertainment from a magician and local bell ringers. The stipulated dress was white tie. It was not until many years after the war that guests discovered that the hosts had been the Evers family. Mr Bryan Evers, a young man at the time of the party, is one of today's Friends of Harvington Hall, and has a fascinating booklet telling the story of the mysterious evening with copies of the invitations and replies and an account of how the evening was secretly organised.

WORLD WAR II AND THE 1940S

AT THE outbreak of war in 1939 the exhibits were put away, and the wall paintings were covered over. The then Curator, Albert Dugard, took a job helping the war effort, and his wife kept the Hall open on three afternoons a week; but in 1942 there were only 642 visitors recorded for the whole year. Early that year, the tea-room was used for classes by an evacuated school from Birmingham. As there was little income, restoration work was suspended until the end of the war.

A letter received in 1996 from Peter Quinn recalls how as a schoolboy he stayed at the Hall and learnt to guide visitors. He also remembers entertaining 'his sweetheart in the barn alongside the moat'! He described the accommodation in the Hall as primitive, but he enjoyed skating on the frozen moat in January 1941. Mr Quinn e-mailed the Hall in 2005 to reminisce about his schooldays.

Records of committee meetings in those years are very enlightening. Topics that were re-visited time and again were fallen plaster in the tea-room, rats in the Hall, the scullery drains, and leaking spouts. Of course there were still no mains connections, water being obtained from the pump in the south garden.

DENIS DUGARD *c1940* ZZZ03262

Here we see Albert Dugard's son, Denis, in his RAF uniform outside the Hall.

On a lighter note the committee regularly undertook to reproduce the Hall guidebooks; the first of them had been written in 1890. As more and more research was undertaken, the books were regularly up-graded – and so was the price, from 6d in 1938 to £3 in 2005.

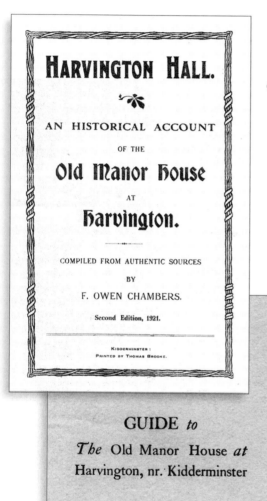

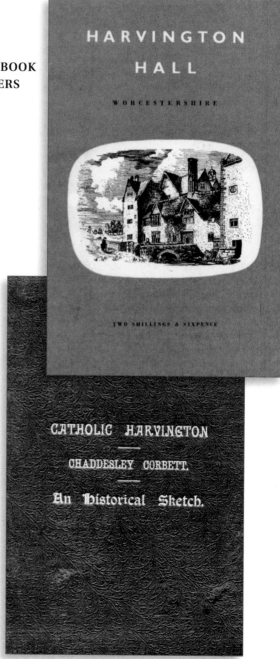

GUIDEBOOK COVERS

Above: **GUIDEBOOK COVERS**

GUIDEBOOK COVER
1965

The 1965 guide had no
pictures in it because
of financial restraints,
but the front cover
showed a blue and
white plate depicting
Harvington Hall.
One of these plates
was seen for sale in
Bloomingdales in New
York in the 1990s.

POSTCARDS *c1930*

The Committee also authorised the sale of post cards; the minutes of 1939 recorded the cost of £10 for 1000 cards including 100% purchase tax.

HH.1   HARVINGTON HALL, NEAR KIDDERMINSTER

HARVINGTON HALL, near Kidderminster.

Harvington Hall—The Withdrawing Room.

HIDING
PLACE

HARVINGTON
HALL
Worcestershire

Left: This postcard shows rather curious views of the hide in Dr Dodd's Library.

Left: This is the spit shaft at the back of the South Room garderobe hide; it was thought that there was an exit from this hide through the shaft, but as the shaft was built after the hide ceased to be used, this is impossible.

HARVINGTON HALL.   THE PULLEY HIDING PLACE

POSTCARDS *c1930*

HARVINGTON HALL, THE GATEWAY HIDING PLACE

Right: Someone's hand is appearing through the hole at the bottom of the Withdrawing Room hide. It used to be thought that this was a secret way of passing food and drink into the hide. It is likely that it is the remains of the mechanism from which the original medieval drawbridge was raised and lowered.

**THE WITHDRAWING
ROOM** *c1965* K16083
(THE FRANCIS FRITH
COLLECTION©)

55

THE KITCHEN *c1965*
K16088

Here we see the Great
Kitchen with the
Brewhouse blocked off.
(THE FRANCIS FRITH
COLLECTION©)

In 1944 Christopher Hussey, the editor of *Country Life*, wrote about the Hall in three different issues, which brought the attention of a much wider audience to the wall paintings and the unusual history of the hiding places. This paved the way for the Hall's later listing as a Grade I historic building (it had already been listed as an Ancient Monument to protect it from use for military purposes during the war).

An annual pilgrimage to Harvington Hall by the Catholic Young Men's Society and their families took place each year in late August, close to the anniversary of the martyrdom of John Wall on 22 August; sometimes the attendance was as high as 600 people, many of whom enjoyed a buffet tea to raise funds for restoration of the Hall.

A special Mass was also celebrated near this date, with a procession across from the church to the Hall. The annual pilgrimage is still held in the garden of the Hall on the first Sunday in September. Over the years Mass has been celebrated in both the front and back gardens at the Hall.

MASS AT THE HALL ON THE FRONT LAWN zzz03280

A SERVICE OF BENEDICTION IN THE BACK GARDEN ON WHAT USED TO BE CALLED THE LARGE COURTYARD ZZZ03282

THE PROCESSION FROM ST MARY'S TO THE HALL ZZZ03281

**AN EARLY
PILGRIMAGE
GATHERING**

ZZZ03279

A pilgrimage on the front
lawn with the Hall Farm
and the old elm tree in
the background.

61

At the end of the war the Hall was still in a fairly basic condition, with no gas or electricity. The committee reports stated that although they would like to have completed the Great Staircase up to the top floor, oak was so scarce that they had to wait until they were given a licence to be able to purchase the required wood.

It was not until 1947 that electricity was laid on to the North Tower, which was the Curator's home, and to the catering kitchen, although earth closets remained in the garden. In 1949 the land in front of the Hall was landscaped to look much as it does today with a half moon lawn and post and chain fencing. Just after the end of the war the visitor numbers were about 4,000 a year.

THE PILGRIMAGE PROCESSION OVER THE SOUTH BRIDGE ZZZ03285

THE 1950S

VISITOR NUMBERS had risen by 1952 to 11,500, and it seemed that the Hall was of interest to many visitors, not just Catholics. However, basic conditions still existed: the curator's most unpleasant task was emptying Elsan buckets into a hole in the north garden. The curator and his wife were the only staff; they had to guide, keep accounts, clean, and cater by themselves for all the visitors, whilst satisfying the committee by keeping up standards.

The Dugard family were followed by several other couples who did not stay long, perhaps for obvious reasons, and eventually the post was taken by Veronica and Lionel Webster, who stayed until 1957.

THE MARBLE ROOM *c1975* zzz03286

Many of the rooms were strewn with sweet smelling flag from the moat to recreate Elizabethan times. Unfortunately, this practice is now considered a health and fire hazard.

In September 1954 Mrs Webster's report to the committee complained of unruly behaviour at the annual ball held in the Great Chamber. She states that 'during the proceedings the staircase hide was invaded and the hinge strained ... and the fire buckets had been used by some of the guests in a most unseemly manner'!

Like curators, Archbishops had also come and gone. Archbishop Masterson, who had followed Archbishop Williams, was himself followed by Archbishop Grimshaw. In 1956 the Historic Building Council gave a grant to the committee which enabled them to put up scaffolding to repair crumbling stonework and re-tile the roofs, to bring the catering kitchen up to date, and to put in a septic tank.

In 1955 undergraduate Michael Hodgetts became a voluntary guide, he went on to be the Hall's Historical Director and in 2005 celebrated 50 years of guiding. Curator Angus Denis Maguire was followed by Bill Williams, and visitor numbers increased in the l960s to 20,000.

THE GREAT CHAMBER *c1965* zzz03283

These photographs were taken as part of a set for a *Country Life* magazine show, and are reproduced with kind permission of *Country Life* magazine.

Opposite top:
THE WITHDRAWING ROOM
zzz03984

Opposite Bottom:
THE TEA ROOM   zzz03983

Above:
THE GATE ROOM   zzz03985

Left:
THE GREAT CHAMBER
zzz03981

Notice how furniture and carpets were moved from room to room for the photographs.

Right: **JUDITH OSBORN** *c1950*

ZZZ03507

Here thirteen-year old Judith Osborn is seen trying out an old horse pistol, which can still be seen on display in the Hall.

Below: **WELCOMING VISITORS** *c1950*

ZZZ03508

Father J Crichton and Mr and Mrs Webster wait to welcome visitors.

Left: **THE HIDE IN THE WITHDRAWING ROOM** *c1950*

ZZZ03495

Mrs Marion Staniford tries out the hide in the Withdrawing Room. Mrs E Ryman, on the left, was an early voluntary guide.

Below: **PREPARING TEAS FOR VISITORS** *c1950*

ZZZ03499

Miss Margaret Hadley, Mrs Mona Hawker and Mrs Vera Hill, with her son David, prepare teas for visitors.

FROM THE 1960s TO THE 1980s

IN THE 1960s, the decision was made to replace the almshouses in Harvington Hall Lane. They had originally been built in the 1700s for Dame Mary Yate, who was a local benefactress. They were, and still are, homes for widows of the parish. The new bungalows were built behind the old cottages which were only demolished when the ladies had moved into their new homes.

THE ALMHOUSES HARVINGTON HALL LANE *1960-61* ZZZ03288

CLOSE UP OF THE PORCHES OF THE OLD ALMHOUSES ZZZ03287

THE ALMSHOUSES *2000* ZZZ03289

**ESTATE COTTAGES
PARK LANE,
HARVINGTON** *c1900*

ZZZ03290

Many cottages that still
surround the Hall, and
others that have long
since been replaced by
modern buildings, were
built for workers on the
estate, which at the time
of Humphrey Pakington
extended to 6000 acres.
See overleaf for a
comparison with today.

Above: **ESTATE COTTAGES PARK LANE, HARVINGTON** *c2000*
ZZZ03291

See previous page for a comparison with the same buildings in 1900.

Left: **STUMP OF ELM TREE** ZZZ03502

The stump of an elm tree on the borders of the Hall car park is a famous landmark. It was once part of an avenue of elms that ran diagonally across the fields towards Woodrow, presumably once the main driveway up to the Hall. Harvington Hall Lane then ran around the back of Harvington Hall Farm instead of in front of it.

In the 1970s and 1980s the committee were still reporting dry rot, woodworm, uneven floors, and inadequate facilities, and it was not until 1983 that the drainage was finally connected to the main sewer. The Hall was still unheated, cleaning was hampered by a lack of power sockets, and the north garden was overrun by long grass, thistles and saplings; visitors to Harvington Hall seemed to tail off, perhaps because its facilities were not up to the standard they had come to expect at other historic properties. The curators during this time were Charles Keefe and his wife, Ivor and Pamela Mortiboy, and Alan and Alicia Cox.

Left: **ELM TREE BEFORE DISEASE CAUSED ITS DEMISE** zzz03503

Below: **MULLIONED WINDOWS IN NEED OF URGENT REPAIR** zzz03292

Above: **IVOR MORTIBOY WITH THE SWINGING BEAM HIDE**
zzz03605

Left: **ALAN COX WORKING WITH SCHOOLCHILDREN IN THE GREAT CHAMBER** zzz03506

ARCHBISHOP MAURICE COUVE DE MURVILLE AND JACQUELINE HYMAN zzz03500
Jacqueline Hyman designed the crewel-work bed hangings and curtains for the Hall.

In 1984 Archbishop Couve de Murville decided that action must be taken, and £100,000 of Diocesan funds was committed to the work. This included the restoration and re-opening of the Georgian chapel with public toilets below it; re-wiring; heat and smoke detectors; a new catering kitchen; new plumbing; the fitting out of the shop in the buttery; and the clearing and opening of the north garden. Mrs Ellen Ryan-Ferris's son Robert, who was created a life peer and took the title of Harvington, donated the money for the re-panelling of two walls of the Great Chamber.

Above: **THE TEA-ROOM** zzz03293

The tea-room was created in the room that is the lower half of the original medieval solar.

Right: **THE TEA-ROOM** zzz03982

THE BREWHOUSE

ZZZ03295

Father Geoffrey
Tucker, parish priest
and chairman of the
committee until 1995, is
seen receiving a cheque
from Bass Brewery
towards the restoration
of the Hall. The barrels
were moved from the
Buttery which now
houses the shop, to the
Brewhouse.

81

THE BUTTERY zzz03294

The butts, which once contained port, were moved from what is now the shop.

Above left: **THE SWINGING BEAM HIDE** zzz03297

Above right: **THE STOOL DISCOVERED IN THE HIDE** zzz03296

The stool in the picture was discovered in the hide hidden by the swinging beam in Dr Dodd's Library. Soon after the picture was taken, the stool was mislaid. However, Father Geoffrey Tucker paid for a replica to be made. It had to be assembled in the hide, as it is too wide to fit through the opening.

Above: **THE CHAPEL**
zzz03986

Left: **HARVINGTON HALL, THE CHAPEL**
c1965 K16087
(The Francis Frith Collection©)

Before the re-opening of the Georgian chapel in the 1980s, Mass was celebrated in the chapel at the top of the Hall. There still are occasional services in the chapel. There are two hides in the attics, one was accessed from above this doorway, but years of restoration have left no trace of the entrance to it.

Above: **THE GEORGIAN CHAPEL**

ZZZ03298

The Georgian chapel re-opened in 1987, and is still used to celebrate Mass every Saturday morning.

Left: **THE HERB GARDEN** *c1950*

ZZZ03300

The Elizabethans had relied heavily on herbs, not only for cooking, but also for medicinal purposes. Mrs Webster had begun to recreate the garden in the 1950s, but constant restoration work and the lack of a downspout had washed it away.

Above left: **THE HERB GARDEN** *2000*

ZZZ03299

The present herb garden was created by volunteers from the Hereford and Worcester Gardens Trust. The letters T, Y and P represent the three families who have owned the Hall, the Pakingtons, the Yates and the Throckmortons.

Above right: **THE NEW LEAD DOWNSPOUT IN THE HERB GARDEN**

ZZZ03604

This matches the one in the courtyard put there 300 years before, and is dedicated to the memory of Archbishop Couve de Murville and his commitment to the Hall. His initials are on the rainwater head.

Below left: **THE NEW RAINWATER TANK** *2000* ZZZ03606

The rainwater tank with the initials of the Hereford and Worcester Garden Trust on it.

THE 1990s

IN THE 1990s, another phase of the restoration was tackled. The Hall had to be closed for 18 months, during which Michael and Rose White acted as caretakers, whilst the administration was carried out firstly by Angie Straker-Nesbitt and then by Denis Tapparo. Denis Tapparo also assisted the newly appointed curators, John and Christine May, on the re-opening of the Hall in 1995. In 1999, Julian Foord took over as curator, and the Business Co-ordinator was Sherida Breeden, later to become the Hall Manager.

THE HALL UNDER REPAIR *1990s* ZZZ03301

THE HALL UNDER REPAIR

1990s zzz03302

Whilst the Hall was closed, it was encased in scaffolding and plastic sheeting, and the stonework, timberwork and roofing were all restored. Mains gas was at last laid on, central heating was installed, and indoor toilets were inserted in the first floor.

As the 20th century drew to a close, the Hall at last had emerged as an historic house that could provide a standard of service that the Archdiocese could be proud of. Schoolchildren were involved in Tudor activities as part of Key Stage 2 studies; there was a summer music festival and an outdoor play; the annual pilgrimage continued; and there were candlelight tours, living history weekends and craft and gift fairs.

Visitors were kept warm and were well looked after; they strolled in beautiful gardens and ate delicious cream teas. But as they had done for a 100 years, they still came primarily to be fascinated, horrified and thrilled by the moving story that unfolded as they were guided from room to room, peering into the dark recesses of hiding places and gazing in wonder at walls that had been decorated 400 years earlier.

At the beginning of the 20th century, Harvington Hall had been within a whisker of being lost. The enormous task that faced the Archdiocese and those early committee members must have seemed nigh on impossible. But gradually, brick by brick, wall by wall, and window by window, they repaired and replaced, until today, at the start of the 21st century, the Hall is a monument to perseverance, not only to the perseverance of those staunch recusant Catholics of the 17th century, but also to the men and women of the 20th century whose diligence and determination have preserved for the future a small glimpse of the past. I am proud to have been one of them.

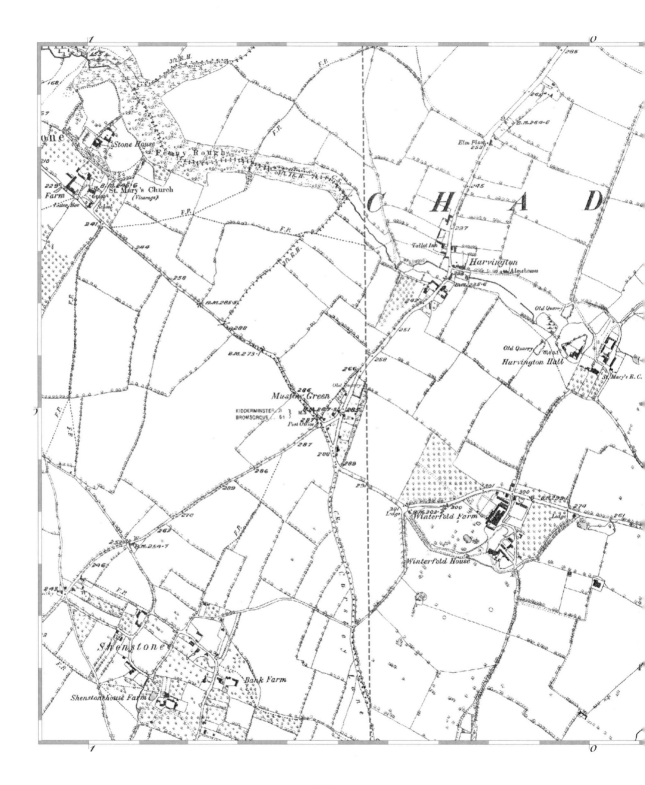

ORDNANCE SURVEY MAP OF CHADDESLEY, SHOWING HARVINGTON HALL
c1900

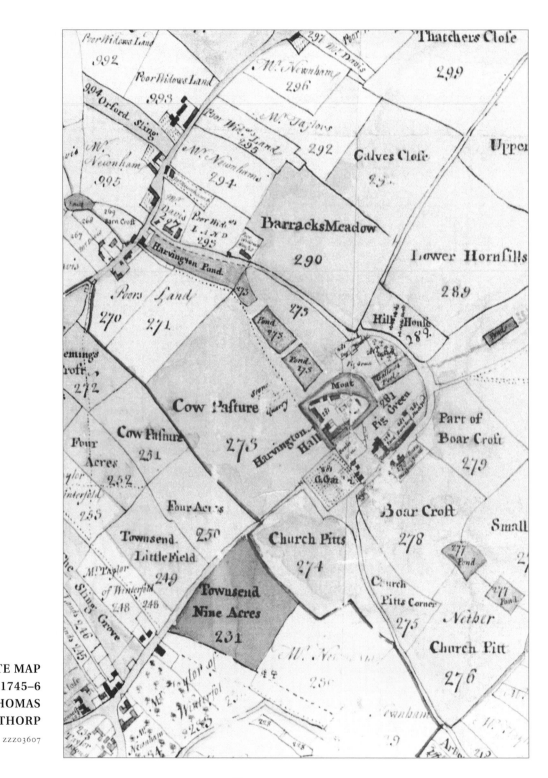

ESTATE MAP
OF 1745–6
BY THOMAS
THORP

ZZZ03607

INVITATION TO HARVINGTON HALL
1879 ZZZ03216

For over a hundred years the Hall has welcomed visitors: here we see an invitation to Harvington Hall in 1879 to celebrate the bicentenary of the death of John Wall. A poem by the local poet Noah Cooke of Kidderminster was read out.

With thanks to the following people who have supplied information or photographs for this book:

The Harvington Hall Management Committee on behalf of the Roman Catholic Archdiocese of Birmingham
Mrs Janet Bartels
Mrs Judith Cunningham
Mr Bryan Evers
Mrs Debbie Oakham

Mrs Jean Rumpsey
Mr Fred Walker
Mrs Jane Yarnold

With thanks to the following for their support and help:

Mrs Mary Fletcher
Mr Michael Hodgetts
Mr Alan Jones
Mr Malcolm Spencer-Williams

SHERIDA BREEDEN ZZZ03494

Sherida is Hall Manager, and compiled this book

INDEX